WITHDRAWN

The Terror of the Snows

The French-Canadian Selection of the International Poetry Forum

THE TERROR OF THE

SNOWS

Selected Poems by
Paul-Marie Lapointe

Translated from the French by
D. G. Jones

University of Pittsburgh Press

Library of Congress Cataloging in Publication Data

Lapointe, Paul-Marie.
  The terror of the snows.

  (Pitt poetry series)
  I. Title.
PQ3919.2.L27A25   841   76–6663
ISBN 0–8229–3327–6
ISBN 0–8229–5274–2 pbk.

The French editions of the books in which these poems first appeared were published by Les Editions de l'Hexagone and are translated here with the permission of the publisher and the poet.

Publication of this book has been made possible by a grant from the United States Steel Foundation.

Contents

Foreword   ix
Introduction   xi

Scene   2

From *The Virgin Burned*
A tiger has a thousand courtesans   7
in the throaty hour of a fleur-de-lys bee   8
stalker of lines   9
ruts filled with the fat hooves of cattle   10
Reflection of still waters   11
A heart inhabited by pink nymphs   12
syrinx charmer of grass snakes   13
In the orchards   14
you were this hand   15
Tall houses   16
night train always on the same track   17
the shepherds sleep in the folds   18
I have already known your rages   19
All shores for me are far away   20
I have an infinity of brothers   21

From *Night of November 15 to 26, 1948*
I love you mine   25

From *Choice of Poems*
Trees   29
Sweet Temptation   35
O Love   36
Birth of the Mosses   37

Wings 1   38
Wings 2   38
We Have Taken Our Places Under the Thunder   39

From *For All Souls*
Each Day   43
Time Falls   44
Day Now Frail as Mica   46
Short Straws   49
Hibernations   55
ICBM   56

From *The Canvas of Love and Other Poems*
hoarse-throated hound   59
the crab of night   60
morning would have to be clawed by a cry   61
Dark Archangel   62
pink is the cave   63
inspired by the triangle   64
the pink the infinitely pink   65
Portrait of a Girl with Brown Hair   66
One   67
full mouth   68
Anonymous Group (Fourth Dynasty)   69
Bone Struck Dumb   70
Scarabs   71
Shore Birds   72
Antonioni (blow-up)   73
Bad Times 1   74
Bad Times 2   74
Vietnam, USA   75
Mission Accomplished   76

Foreword

The hope of the International Poetry Forum is to be no less international than poetry itself. To be sure, such a hope invites certain practical limitations. While poetry has the destiny of speaking to all men at all times, the International Poetry Forum concerns itself with bringing particular poets into contact with as many people as possible right now. While poetry speaks ultimately from and to the common nationality of flesh and blood, the International Poetry Forum attempts in a proximate way to permit poets of different nationalities and alphabets to have their work known and understood by people of nationalities and alphabets other than their own.

To help achieve this goal the International Poetry Forum has initiated a series of foreign selections. These selections provide for the publication of American translations of some of the works of foreign poets and the distribution of such books throughout the United States, Europe, and the poets' homelands.

The Terror of the Snows by Paul-Marie Lapointe is the eighth in this series, the first seven having been the Turkish Selection (*Selected Poems* by Fazıl Hüsnü Dağlarca, translation by Talât Halman) in 1968; the Syria-Lebanon Selection (*The Blood of Adonis* by Adonis, or Ali Ahmed Said, translation by Samuel Hazo) in 1971; the Swedish Selection (*Windows and Stones* by Tomas Tranströmer, translation by May Swenson) in 1972; the Israeli Selection (*A Canopy in the Desert* by Abba Kovner, translation by Shirley Kaufman) in 1973; the Jamaican Selection (*Uncle Time* by Dennis Scott) in 1973; *Eskimo Poems from Canada and Greenland* (translation by Tom Lowenstein) in 1974; and the Greek Selection (*The Axion Esti* by Odysseus Elytis, translation by Edmund Keeley and George Savidis) in 1974.

Essential to the task of bringing this selection of Paul-Marie Lapointe's poems to the attention of American and English readers have been the contributions of Naim Kattan of the Canada Council, which sponsored the translation, and James Hosey of the United States Steel Foundation, which funded the publication itself.

Samuel Hazo, *Director*
International Poetry Forum

Introduction

The director of the News and Public Affairs Service of the French radio network, Radio-Canada, Paul-Marie Lapointe, has spent most of his active life as a journalist, first in Quebec City, then in Montreal. But he has also become, in the judgment of fellow poet Yves Préfontaine, the strongest, most incisive, most essential voice in Quebec poetry. In 1972, Lapointe won both Quebec's Prix David and Canada's Governor General's Award for his work as a poet.

The most reticent of moralists and the gentlest of revolutionaries, he has yet written that any vital poem is both a moral act and an act of revolt. Insofar as Eros is the motor of art and, as Freud maintained, civilization is a repressive anxiety structure, this is bound to be the case. The morality of the poet, said Wallace Stevens, is the morality of sensation—a view that would have been heretical enough in the Jansenist Quebec of Lapointe's youth and that remains heretical in the contemporary world. For though it may not exhibit the puritanical morality of an older Quebec, the modern world is nonetheless oppressive, certainly more violent, and—as Lapointe's news-gathering service would attest—not unjustly acclaimed the Age of Anxiety. In the wintry climate of Quebec or the contemporary world, in the confrontations between ideology and art, between the intellectual security of dogma and the sensuous risk of the poem, between power and intransigence and fraternity and accommodation, Lapointe's poetry has always spoken for the latter and been subversive like the sun.

Paul-Marie Lapointe exploded into poetry with over a hundred poems all written toward the end of his first (and last) year as a student of architecture at the Ecole des Beaux-Arts in Montreal. Revised in the fall, they were published before the year was out as *Le Vierge incendié* (1948), *The Virgin Burned* or, perhaps, *Virgo Burned Up.*

Lapointe was born a Virgo in 1929, and he grew up in St-Félicien near Lac Saint-Jean, a hundred and fifty miles north of Quebec City. It is an area famous for its blueberries—three make a pie—and, as Lapointe once remarked with reference to his title, for its forest fires. It is also the country of *Maria Chapdelaine*, a classic Quebec novel by Louis Hémon dramatizing the traditional Quebec culture. Rural, French, and Catholic, it had little interest in the myth of progress, in the stock market or its failure. Life was centered on the parish and organized around the recurring rhythms of the land, the family, the ritual church year. It was a world where, according to *Maria Chapdelaine*, nothing changed, ever. Lapointe's education, first at the Séminaire de Chicoutimi during the last years of the war, then at the Collège Saint-Laurent in Montreal, no doubt reflected the climate of this traditional culture.

In such a context *The Virgin Burned*, with its profusion of images, irreverent, unpredictable, often erotic, arrived with something of the violence of the spring breakup. The poems reveal an exuberant delight in language and a spontaneous mixture of ironic irritation and lyric affirmation. Organized in associational clusters, they increasingly abandon conventional form and syntax. In both form and theme, they were entirely new in Quebec literature.

The overall thematic movement may be suggested by the section titles of the book: "Scalped Heads," "Your Sleek Bellies," "They Lay Waste My Heart," "There Are Dreams," and "Creation of the World." In its underlying image of an old order razed, as a virgin forest may be swept by fire so that new life may spring up green, in its celebration of the sensuous body of the world, in its suggestion that language and art are arms in the imaginative re-creation of one's world, the book anticipates the major themes of a generation of Quebec poetry.

If Lapointe's first book reflects something of the comedy of spring, his second, *Choice of Poems* (1960), reflects the romance of summer. But, as we can see, it took nearly a decade to arrive.

World War II had greatly accelerated changes in the traditional life of Quebec and had brought to Montreal a variety of publishers, painters, and writers—notably André Breton and the surrealist program, creating an unprecedented cultural ferment. But at the end of the war a reaction set in. When the painter Paul-Emile Borduas published, also in 1948, a surrealist-inspired manifesto, *Total Refusal*, rejecting both the traditional Quebec culture and that of modern technological society, he lost his job at the government-supported art school where he taught. The decade that followed under the regime of Maurice Duplessis has been referred to, especially by writers, as the Great Darkness.

By the time Lapointe's *Choice of Poems* appeared in 1960, however, Quebec was on the brink of the so-called Quiet Revolution, which during the sixties was to transform the traditional culture radically and, for good or for ill, make Quebec part of the modern technological world. The poems signal the new, more expansive climate, and in them we find fully developed two of the main themes of the sixties, the celebration of love and of the land.

The magnificent poem "Trees," inspired by a government publication on the trees of Canada and written in a single burst one Sunday morning, is both one of the most richly detailed celebrations of the land and life of Quebec and an adventure into the world of total metaphor, where pastoral becomes apocalypse. Into the basic litany of trees, Lapointe weaves a host of free associations which integrate the human and the natural worlds to conclude the poem with a single image of a cosmic tree, its nests full of children.

Lapointe's earliest mentors were Rimbaud and Eluard. Others he has mentioned include Whitman and Lorca, Neruda and Guillen. But "Trees" may suggest that Lapointe is perfectly serious when he speaks of the influence of jazz musicians—John Coltrane, Miles Davis—with their emphasis on improvisation.

The last section of the volume, particularly "We Have Taken Our Places Under the Thunder," reflects a totally different climate, which dominates his next book, *For All Souls* (1965). If the Quebecker no longer has to contend with the problems of an overly static culture, he must now contend with those of change that renders him almost catatonic: the world of the rat race and the arms race, the Cold War and the atom bomb, continuous dislocation and violence. Winter brings a satirical edge to Lapointe's vision. Man is seen giving himself up, in smugness or in terror, to the cold, to the forces of division, aggression, and death. He becomes a "stupefied family." His guardian angel peers through a bombsight. "Time Falls" and "ICBM" are among Lapointe's most explicit and public poems and probably speak most immediately to the reader, in or out of Quebec.

The irony of these poems is tempered by an elegiac concern for the souls, albeit mainly of the dead, and perhaps for those fleeting glimpses we get of summer, of birds, and of girls. Lapointe is not by temperament a satirist, but rather what Robert Graves called a Muse poet. Even the mysterious divinity he evokes and would serve, welling like water among the stones, or like suns bleeding warmth into a frigid universe, is more feminine than masculine.

This bias is more evident in "Short Straws," a series of eighteen poems remarkable for their attempt to hold summer and winter in a tense balance, for their often simultaneous evocation of terror and love, for their extreme speed and concision.

In the latest volume, *Tableaux de l'amoureuse* (1974), rather freely translated here as *The Canvas of Love and Other Poems*, that difficult balance tends to be broken. As if by a kind of natural recoil, Lapointe returns in the first two sections, nearly half the volume, to evoke and to celebrate the vital warmth, the regenerative power, of woman, of Eros. He does so with a new intensity and a sometimes curious combination of intimacy and distance. Then with a short, mixed, rather unusually occasional series of poems on Egypt, the tone modulates back toward winter, the dominant climate of the final section and of poems such as "Bad Times," "Vietnam, USA," and "Mission Accomplished." If there is a new note here it may be in the hint of autumn, with its melancholy but also its suggestion of a solidarity in death as in life, which is quite different from the ironic desolation of man's own violence.

The climate of the poems, of the world, has become increasingly hostile. Only the metals remain serene—and in "Short Straws," even they are menaced, to say nothing of man, the birds, or the tree, that recurring feature of Lapointe's poetry. In one of the latest poems, the birds taking sudden flight trace on the air the pattern of a black seal, of a tree burned black in the midst of time. Yggdrasil, World Tree. One would prefer to suppose that like the forest of Lac Saint-Jean after a fire, it too will become newly green.

Nothing is simple, says Lapointe at the end of the latest volume, and he is not likely to cultivate the cynical simplicity of the fatalist.

Lapointe's whole concern in poetry has been to resist such simplicities. He has always put the emphasis on the first draft, on the spontaneous, on improvisation. He has resisted the trap of discursive logic, linear syntax, even of his own image. Rather than pursue a conceit or extend a metaphor, he would destroy the initial image. The poem explodes like a seed and ramifies. More accurately, perhaps, it is a series of luminous tracks that betray the invisible electrons startled from their atomic sleep. Lapointe would remain faithful to the ambiguity, the indeterminacy, of the moment of experience. And with luck, the elliptical movement of the poem should retain something of its unpredictability, its mysterious coherence, its force.

The short poem "Scene," which is taken from the latest volume and is reproduced here in the original French as well as in translation, may very well serve as an illustration of Lapointe's strategy and, I think, its success. For we may make all kinds of large statements about the climate of the world, about life and about death, and yet not attain the kind of conviction a poem has when it succeeds in finding, in the curve of its rhythms and the structure of its images, its own internal coherence, its resonance and evocative life. It then puts us in touch with something vital and creative, in the writer, in ourselves, in the world. Of the poet, what more can we ask?

D. G. JONES

Scène

heurté
le fourreau déploie ses lames

dans la biche la féminine
s'animent les sept langues de l'hydre

l'eau bouge
rapide effeuillaison du soleil

oubli double

au pied de l'étang
seul
un saule retient le vent

Scene

Scene

struck
the sheath unfolds its blades

in the doe the feminine
quickening the Hydra's seven tongues

the water stirs
rapid exfoliation of the sun

double oblivion

at the bottom of the pond
alone
a willow still holds the wind

From *The Virgin Burned*

A tiger has a thousand courtesans
in his claws   a thousand tongues
a thousand wombs of gardens
in the nape of his neck
Poppies of hair in the hand-
clasped day
in the sleepless night
of open palms

Trembling of his whole body
Flat-chested dawns of snow
without love   without fire
without question flat as the mouth
fixed on the stale meat

Gingham girls   girls of night
lily white bed bright
All unites the rough and brown
bodies to the neck's luxurious
peach down with the veins
zebra-striped

Men with the hooves of wild beasts—
what's left of the siesta
trunks of date palms—
tucked away for a furry snack
tucked away for a feathery sleep
A heart of gooseflesh

in the throaty hour of a fleur-de-lys bee I rest on the ceiling of sleep   the kimono yaps in the mirror light   looking-lamp hand on the belly and stained-glass mouth in the clouds   the watercolor wafts a great balloon of lotus blossoms over the leaves of the temple   but now that I have my nails in your cheeks as a fan in the temples more tender a piano the waking of such troubled eyes on my knee in the desert   now yesterday stalker of lines consumed by round mouths I dine on red and green drawings. I have love packed in my thighs; love full-horned, old goat. They will have known the deep wound of the throbbing sex. Poor unexpected reddening of the goddess, suddenly deep down in their legs full of worms. They have their toes well stuck in the clay, and the full sun of the Hindu carvings. I'm going to wait up for the fall of the world spewed out by the trumpets; by the remorse of the rams. The Ariadnes, their hair flying but suffering, claw at themselves, Erinyes' nails on the swollen nerve. The squared paper takes on the undulations of eyes joined by feathers. Papier-mâché dreams strung together with the worst of the bad books. The wise men with their external eyes take note of the heretical alms, but so much more sculptural than the seminal offerings of round priests. It is pleasant to commit a cloud on the strict face of a plaster saint.

ruts filled with the fat hooves of cattle started up again by the
nauseous stars   diamond compact of the whole day's sweat   I de-
serve a sweet sleep in the pits   mouths devour the sun falling in
tears   eyelids sealed against the blue noon with the holy candle
of a spare dried-up angel   it rains from the window agonizing pain
the yellow of magpies' beaks   claw hooked in the worm   bodies in
the plumage of white crows   people with slack flesh and the phan-
toms of the newborn   yet the river of bodies among the tangled
boats and cadavers   the wind full of gay fish   the warmth of dying
again   the breast's delight in the nape's fingers   seaweed in the
mouth of rearing capes   rage in the wanton leg too much a woman
beach-head reduced by the pines you on the make beside the rotted
rafts devour the yellow butterflies with the cheeks of your ass

Reflection of still waters on the smooth belly. Stained glass of the sorcerer of kneeling pieties; good girl of the vineyards. A worldly saint in acrobatic trim would work with nothing less. One scene with the lustful devil had her stretched out naked among serpents very becoming in their coiled skins. Enough of these orgies of blond seraphim all hairy down to the torso itself, and at the navel the really animal odor of a small snake!

A heart inhabited by pink nymphs, lesbian festivals. Great wild-eyed race round the circus of gothic grapevines and sickening gods. Days of running the high noons of pleasure; death smudging the little warblers in the tulips; crushing the palms on tearful sands; feet of thorns in the skin. Deep rivery sleep, without barges without voluptuous airs. The wings of the knees and thighs skim over water lilies. Village that dies, like a cry, from height to height, and the two banks of waves lapping along the edge of the belly.

syrinx charmer of grass snakes   paradoxical saw-toothed flute
reedy satyr   feverish eel   o shaggy with love fascination of veins
in the streams of running gas   paper snakes of rhythm and Bacchus
imprinted on temples through the balls of the feet   sea urchins in
aquariums   spiky hair full of slugs and the sea's rollers   barnacles
    gulls   hippocampi

In the orchards
the noonday monsters forgot us
because they were blind
or could no longer sniff us out

So we set forth to lay hold
of the crystal future
the castle gleaming with every hope
streaming like watered silk

And already the most nimble
sprung from their furry hide-outs
the hundred-limbed monkeys
and the whole troop
we went running one after the other
single file we are free

But an invisible vulture
unsuspected
swallowed subito the snake

you were this hand   this gentle stroll in the hollows of the neck at
evening   the patchwork gardens and the houses at the corner of
the eye   all landscapes are behind the houses   hairy mountains
kisses on the breasts when it rains   it's autumn the wind that tears
you from the tree of sleep   we have sundered loves and rhubarb
hands   we have closed pages exhausted bodies   it's going to snow
    it's a matter of dying with the flower beds   we will become the
white noise of the void   watching the water move in the icy mirror
    we know the way   it comes to us all at once   when the sun is
dead no one wants to die any more   where to go when we've been
so much at home with the trees and the animals

Tall houses   I crawl my only son
sang the three nuns   you drive me crazy
I've had enough my pretty puss   I say
man belches in the black bath   my grass
is pink   I am your drunken boy
who deguts you   we wanted it too much
even so it wasn't worth the price
still you're not bad and it keeps me going

night train always on the same track always dragging me back by
the hair   I've left my quiet village with the lamps in the window
and the untroubled sleep of the wicker cradles   night train with its
baggage cars its chests of tears and the eyes of the terminal in my
brow   they sleep   those who travel walk in their sleep   there's
this one head in his arms   departure's head   the other has his feet
against the whirling pane of the landscape   exiles abandoned to
prolonged stops and those with ties with their baggage   and this
heart that takes up the whole place we haven't taken

the shepherds sleep in the folds of the most untroubled sleep
dreamed of by chatterbox   the horn waited for no moon to split
no tits torn by piano teeth   no cry of passion in the evening rotten-
apple district   the dog ranges along the crest of black trees in the
liquor rich with wolf-faced howls   but I sleep   lamb's fleece in
the ring of my fingers   pink face of silence with its soft look
these have been for an hour mauve peignoirs   they have put to
sleep the fevers in the cushions   the passing guilts tails between
their legs have been chased off by hearts   needle cries in the woolly
lounging   carnage is seated by the river   the breath of the sea
walks the carp in grassy pastures and the wall dreams of a man easy-
chair skull where a small bear tired of the day's accountings smokes

I have already known your rages
the fierce swell sweeping your throat
now that all grows drowsy again
now that you recall who I am
along with the hands of flowers
the butterflies of summer
the trees in the rooms

I have tasted your plum tears
your plums from white prisons
where the black rabbits
leapt like hearts

After today tomorrow's
embarcations in the islands
are moored to the keys of your nape
the twenty fingers eaten
by the mists along the shores
by the manticores

One mustn't forget
we forget to leave when we've left
one mustn't cry without crying
for having failed to depart
one day when a great ship
whispered in our ear
now is the time to depart

All shores for me are far away
and the buoys of hope
sunk in the morning
lost in the distance

the flat table of the sea
the wall battered in by eyes
the eyes of Iroquois decked in linen
the eyes of sluts with the muzzles of angels

all this is going to grow
in the crystal spruces
walking in the park
their hands behind their backs
despite the wild raids of horns
despite the legs of the pretty girls
and the love in the policeman's nightstick

all this my bright armor
my dark weaponry   arms of my house
beside the sea of incantations
beside the sea of lamentations

I have an infinity of brothers
I have an infinity of sisters
and I am my father and my mother

I have the trees   the fish
the flowers and the birds

The roughest kiss
the most baffled act
the killer with no knife
is pierced with light

But the corrosion will never reach
my iron realm
where the hands are so dried up
they lose their leaves

The faïence bursts out laughing in the stucco
the icy sky
the many-faced sun which no longer appears
Brothers and sisters
my thousands of adamant stars

From *Night of November 15 to 26, 1948*

I love you mine
give me the cuff the mass
the cope of the tiger
the expert Amazonian riders quivering with paint
and powdered rumps at bay without fox
without hare
I've been losing my life in the forests
but some day
I will find you again
the one never before encountered
but that I know to be mine
on the strength of a big book
of the misty key of faith

From *Choice of Poems*

Trees

I write tree
tree spinning rings into cones sap into light
roots of the rain and of fair weather   animate earth

pine   the white and the red   Norway and jack pine
tough heavy-wooded pine   pine with long twisting needles
winter squash and saplings
pitch pine   dwarf and rock   lordly pine
   pine with tender pores   pines traversing time
   wrapped in their snows   proud masts stretched
   sails dry-eyed and remorseless   armed companies
pines of quiet cupboards   of simple houses
wood for tables and for beds
wood for paddles frames and beams   men's bread
   rising in your squared palms

cedars of Lebanon   swamp cedar and arbor vitae   white
   cedar   polished arms   yellow cedar cupressa nootka-
   tensis   a windfall of dressmaker's needles   junipers
   red cedar redolent cedar shakes   hope-chest panels of
   warmth

juniper keeping the plumb of alphabets

Norway spruce   black   white   prairie spruce
nailed down   summer's
spruce beer   spiny spinet and upright   wild drum

balsam and fir   white   red   concolor and graceful
   gigantic   timbers for Babel   coiffeur for all
   seasons   pole beams for fantasy towns

locomotive blistered stack   roofing of mines
fir   candle of childhood

evergreen cornucopias   prickly tribes   evergreen
   crests of the morning   deep-sea divers of the

wind   evergreen Don Quixotes unhorsed except for
their mountains   raised trumpets splitting the
heavens   conifers   petrified flames   burning
greens   frozen fire   evergreens
vertical spines of fish eaten by birds

I write tree
tree for the tree

birch   the yellow birch ripple-grained   weeping
    birch   cherry birch   birch   the flowering
    mulberry sweet-smelling   red   white birch
    birch branching grass snakes   leafing fine
    gears   disengaged   housebreaker hidden in
    poplar leaves   slipping arms through the cage
    of the weathers   caging birds   caging the wind

birchbark cleaving the water of rivers
foundry iron and type font   winter fountain   frozen
    jet   fine parquetry   evening fireside   entasis
    of towers and balls
sleeping albatross

sapwood between dark and dusk
sapwood between dawn and lantern light

I write tree
tree for the trunk and its leaves
tree for the fern of the fallen soldier   his limestone
    memorial and the bird that takes flight with a cry

tree
poplar   false aspen   large-toothed trembling aspen
    wolf willow   worrisome griffin   immobile
    dredger of moss and earth   narrow-leaved poplar
    low-browed scrub poplar   upright Lombardi poplar
    dry old hack   rancid blinkers

balm of Gilead   embalmer of tears   poplar with
   spear-shaped buds   cottonwood   pussy willow
   nonmedicinal swabs   and catkins   bird's-foot of
   small rachitic birds   matchsticks   windbreakers
   of the forest   bodyguards and barrel makers
   winter's white coal

tree
tree for the tree and the Huron
tree for the hunter and tree for the hatchet
tree for the siren and tree for the wheat   cargo ship
   cart horse

nutwood   Circassians   masseurs of the blue   nutwood
   with long fruit   walnut and butternut   happily
   nutty nutwood   nuggets enlightened from within
   makers of bowls   aerial yachts   etchings

bitterbark willow   willow whose thin lashes break
   like speech on the air   plumed peahen and
   fugitive fleet-footed peacock   black willow
   willow with peach leaves   willow with mortal
   leaves   crackwillow white and weeping willow
   trappings of the dead

hickory nut ovular black and bitter   shellbark
   hickory   nuts pierced in the quick   swamp
   hickory or bitter pignut   shagbark   sporting
   hickory   springy butts

hornbeam hardwood ironwood   narcissistic diver
   wet egotist with stifled cry

alder   tigalder   alder with burls   hairy-branched
   headless tortoises   failed ray fish   frail alder
   with studs   black enameler   slim-leaf alder

long-stemmed glasses   shriveled dwarf alder
antennae torn from an insect

tree

the tree is nail and is cross
crosstie and watermark
crossbar   sword hilt   gunstock
bombsight   telephone   blast furnace   telegraph
aluminum and neon cross
skyscraper and doghouse   torturer's rack and hunger's
    bare board

muscular oaks   mastiffs gendarmes percherons   oaks
    with great seeds   photographers and sunflowers
    heads of Franciscans   acorns   white oak or swamp
    oak or quercus bicolor as the fit decides or
    nothing decides

curly-leaved white or blue   oak boom tie on the
    polished bowsprit   mosaic chinquapin

arctic oak   oak trunk autumn labor   scarlet oak
    kissing oak   swamp oak spreading like a slow
    fire in the south
builder   heavy transport of thirst   habitable block
    tan of hides and of beaches

beechnut with open husks   beech mast feathery nuptials
    chestnut   horse chestnut   fruiterer given to flights
    of streaked fancy
beech filters for vinegar   vats for aging liqueurs

I write tree
tree   wood for the otter and the black bear
wood for woman and for fox

black cherry   long-lasting October cherries
    cherries and tiny wild cherries   chokecherries
    and wild   cherries for jam   heady brandy-colored
    cherries   nipples of amorous women

chicot   gymnocladus   locust with long pods
    palettes for the picaresque brush

sumac   handsome-leaved   staghorn sumac   phallic
    flower among rocks and in sandy soil

three-leaved alder   brother of the hops

elm   shy steel   luminous wood   utilitarian elm
    elm with egg-shaped leaves   saw-toothed chewers
    of the wind   slippery elm   wych elm rock elm
    uncertain arms   arms of cider and feeble frames

rose tree
hips and moss

cherry   plum tree   hawthorn bush
sorb apple   wild
crab apple   artists in silverpoint and flowering spit
    little girls in amorous wretchedness

decorators   magnolias   tulip trees   sassafras wise
    kings of the Orient   caravan drivers laden with
    aromatic herbs   censer   soap dish

witch hazel stanching the blood of wounds

sorb apple for birds   rowanberry   service tree
    maskouabina bitter and polar drawing the lover
    to the intimate embrace

apple sweet-toothed muncher

I write tree   gentle animals   wild   domestic
suety ash   ash with elder leaves
the lime or linden   midnight's infusion

maples with multiple keys   parachute corps of
    winged samara

striped maple   moose maple   summer provisions
    faithful to game tracked to bush and bracken
    fire maple   silver maple   blue-veined temples
    of girls
ash-leafed maple   box elder   growing like laughter
    and born on the run
sugar maple   maple spring

blue elderberry   larkspur bluebird meadowlark
    whistle through the fingers

trees

the trees are crowned with children
keep warm their nests
are loaded with fine flour
hunger sleeps in their shade
and smiles multiply their leaves

Sweet Temptation

to what do the flowers succumb
and your breasts

to the sun to the night
to my hands' caress
to the spell of perfumes
to the sweet temptation to sleep between the pages of a book

O Love

o love
my wintergreen
berries tufting to the sun

o love
health recaptured beyond walls and such the open ground
　　inhabited solely by your flesh violet-veined invades
　　my heart　　o open one

o love
my wintergreen

Birth of the Mosses

spiders orisons pretty feet
weave the veils of virgins
wing ensnared
wing-lit angel
the flows of granite dream
by the lily's head
with its palace guard of pistils
the pollens finesse of flowers rouge
envelop me
o arms o ankles

the birth of the mosses was cried aloud
plucked guitars
in the animal-muted evenings

Wings 1

there's no touching this round bird
this navel
without its raising around itself
the pink cage of its fingers

Wings 2

in the armpits nests
are hung to which
at night to sleep
there come wings
of warmth

We Have Taken Our Places Under the Thunder

we have taken our places under the thunder
frail shell of abandon
in the delicate warmth of the first glass on
    the autumnal fountains
in the crepitations of silence and of the tree
behind the screen of the hoarfrost

we have taken our places under the thunder
at the heart of the earth
in the ramifying terror of picks and of hammers
in the net of the sirens
prisoners of the hours and of arms

we have taken our places under the thunder

companions are frightened their breasts will go white
words become lime

their upright skeletons shoulder the winter

the sign of the lightning marks men
                              from one day to the next

we have taken our places under the thunder
desolate planet
despite the rivers and capes
despite the perennial forests

the capitals trample their people

From *For All Souls*

Each Day

each day an assassinated earth inters its men
thundering sun
jealous of the different species
and the gyrations of weak widows

each day anyhow a planet
above all in February year-long month
shoves its ashes in my face
my city is alarmed

and the oasis always
of a sharp intransigence
sows the disaster of its tender leafing stones

against the honey
against the sweetness of capsizing in the hour
the rude angel of despair

Time Falls

(the earth is our menace

at the corner of the street, each noon,
  the same well-fed face
the assurance of the passing parade
the fanfare
and all the dead that hole in the heart . . .)

time falls
　　　　families showers gusts of sparrows
time falls

　　　　a lost tribe floats up to the surface
　　　　children of the pyramids of the sun
　　　　amphoras of dust corn and furs
　　　　cliffs of dead
　　　　(cliffs like hives from which the gorged
　　　　　souls of the death eaters the whites
　　　　　take wing)
　　　　stupefied family

time falls
　　　　Abenaki Maya Birmingham Negro
　　　　civil souls of my dead savages
　　　　anger interred in the dung heap
　　　　　of horses of prey

　　　　in the knowledge of soldiers and saints
　　　　in the armed frigates
　　　　for the swooning delight of an infanta and
　　　　　the pathos of a tribute to the unknown
　　　　　soldier

time falls

       in the month of the salmon the villages
         are installed the municipal offices
       the fishermen and anglers
       the capitals polished with death's hand

time falls

       slave galleys
       Atahualpa
       today's savages
       wiped out
       (Cinderella palpitating in silk her three
         square meals her prince
       O peaceful sleep
       round earth where the houses all alike
         hug each other
       the final rest may come from one day to the next)

time falls

       the small men of prehistory eddy
       between the buildings
       in the rain freighted with missiles

time falls

       satisfied species

Day Now Frail as Mica

day now frail as mica when the puddles rot
a winter's anemones   desirable sun

> father you are peopled with wood chips
> a river of rigid fish
> swallows   crosses hung in the heart
>   of the villages

> there are no more leaves

> but with all the wood you order
> with the cities all lit up
> where are we going?

the metal flakes in the light
>   voracious compost to rescind the flesh
>   and memory itself

dust from the wood dust from the fire your blindness
   keeps watch
carpenter bound for death

your fellow men are busy splicing rope
>   o ship hung high and dry
loves cradled there if the night does not seize and
   toss them out
braying to the sun

the dead and the living

futile husbands of the gulfs and the capes where the
   mothers set out to give birth to time and lost it

for children cast in the cells by hope
>   the very arteries of the malediction pray
>   to the black night to knot them to
>   twist them to slice them up

for the children working on rage
  the cells accumulate stupid patience its
   throat slit resignation people on their
   knees

for the children delivered of their mothers
  the motionless altars croaking with the
   menace of gravestones honeysuckle
   and kept ideas long fondled by the
   pious hands among the stones

for the children left to their own devices
  tied hand and foot the capital cities
   the laws sealed lips and condescending
   blades servilities

your breath withheld daily attempt to domesticate
 death
like annihilating earth
   (thus the diver caresses—provokes—
    the temptation to be possessed finally
    by the water or endlessly to outleap
    space, dismembered, dumb, to the point
    of not being)

but the members for shouting out
for bringing the steel to the ground
but the members for loving

where are we going? cedar hedges heated houses

skins of lovers who shiver in the sidereal wind among
 occupied lands
the masters admire you
  like pieces of porcelain
their caprice wipes you out

the voices are shoveled under
the protests are throttled from day to day more faint
and vain

soon the silence will be no more than the cry of the
    first of all the dead

Short Straws

1

they crumble in my skin the fragile earth
its plants

sprung from these and fire its minerals

the entire geology

2

the flower only enters the girl haunted by death
to articulate there a fragility

she fears a village may be blotted out
by fire
its men its houses
gardens in stone

pernicious season under threat of death

3

feast year
you have all the weight of a kiss
a star gone nova with a cry

4

divinity lying in wait
hidden among the rocks
falling like an apple from the tree
or bursting forth o geyser to suddenly
once upon a time or tomorrow
seize you by the throat

mystery of earth

5
love's respiration fills
the space of night
as would a tiny sea
whose islands alternately swell and shrink
as on their sands wash tides
of anguish or neglect

6
soar above me asteroid

the mouth I love salutes you from a spring where
    the fern disputes the intransigence of being
    loved throughout one's life like a bouquet or
    still more tenderly of being whelmed by tears
    the sea

7
the sea a crystal
(I survey it from the air)
transparency moving
currents of warmth manual
fluidities of wind

it comes from the other end of the world
retaining of continents and islands
only light and those
still wetted down with love

8
as by rain
or passion
I am swept by a music full of tears

angry loving
beaten out by the jungle weighted down by chains
working the whip

more supple than a woman in the midst of love
and like her piercing itself through and through

turning the whole world upside down

uttering cries

9
in the clay the white archetypal lover
in the limestone the tender spacing of her bones
in the plumage of a bird

planetary shiver of love

10
distress o black lady

pavilion of cries archangel folding under
    the burden of rain
night crisscrossed with terror's knives

distress like a heart

the hips beat trajectory of stifled earth
I shall sleep in the terrified stress
of alloys locked

into high speeds

11
birth of green

she covers the passing world with trembling attention
kindling in her branches little passionate fires
whole families of suns

bark's taste no longer suffices no more contains
my blood my ardor

summer's rigid tenderness

12
small rain of ordinary men
I greet you

like the coming of a fifth season

13
the chicks peck about in the dirt

this rhythm cannot be sustained
imminent terror

the concrete makes firm its position
to sacrifice to the gods
every revolt act of resistance

medusas are piled on display in the sun

14
a great body feeds the city with birds
long sessions coifed with lifted hands
where ease prepares indulgences

a solid beast and hardly voracious
he asks only to be gnawed on
every spring whereby the warmth is released
and man from within

the sounds of music assail us
thus we satisfy
the lukewarm cannibals   the bowels of desire

we savor in the velvet of reliquaries
bonified mortal women
with melting thighs

tigresses
their sobs

15
the teal spins sun into a call
a trawl to net the summer
a birdcage for the sea
                    where girls will come to tan
                    their salty knees

16
I piece together wisdom for my sons
carnivorous architectures
that the families of their thoughts will shelter there
raise angels animals

in the breaking of the parallels
in the coupling of beams and the light
make them domestic

tears that water carries off to far interiors
the former villages
the most respectable ancestors
and the divinity that from the depths of time
   has never ceased
to well up between the stones

17
in the grip of the lady of light
the saddened mallard takes to his wings

that having so delighted the lakes
he should disappear to more torrid zones
such is the terror of the snows

18
as the rock its crystal vein
and the girl her arteries
anguish polishes its ground

Hibernations

within you I let fly white birds

few birds are white apart from doves
unless they've wintered here
planted like crosses in such space
a dry unfolding a deployment of shivers
as strange as the snow itself
has it we ask one care except to perch on us

on the villages
on the cages

between the stones the straws sculptured by the wind

our dead do not fly off
unless within ourselves

as do the children we have
who beat out paths to the interior

white birds   and airy skeletons

ICBM

each day astonished you land up on earth
this night was not the last

but the brontosaurus
and Caesar
and the Incas
and the Crow circling

watery world

the craters erupt
    embryonic cry

the Cloud like a toad squats on its earth
squeezes it with small repeated hugs

the mother of dust

the wild goose makes it from the Andes in spite of the radar

on nylon catwalks flung
between worlds
sway the delicate haunches of girls

watery world welter of corpses

day breaks bad but I know in getting through it
    it is not the last

a bombardier stretches out at your side
your nights are secure!

O President O Good Shepherd
General of the Islands and of the Moons

the children curl up like burnt leaves

From *The Canvas of Love and Other Poems*

hoarse-throated hound tracked by death toward the
    abyss of blood that was its master
the black bull whose pierced brow lowers at the moon
    softly complexioned and circled with red
lovely sweet-smelling flesh appearing in a sky to be
    made of the same stuff as the sun—just as
    the naive paintings picture it—
yellow as the heart of the buttercup
in contrast to the three pools from which the robins
    rise up
taking a pattern of flight whose precise and complicated
    trace has the form of a black seal
of a tree burnt black in the midst of time

in the space thus defined
around which there gathers the presence of terrible clouds
the howl withheld of the very humble
his imminent destruction

that against which no god rises up
neither the hot armies we have ourselves raised
    in the disaster
to protect ourselves from the opprobrium and the
    machinations of living

the crab of night has no such hold as we thought
over passion
the vampire of eternity has not torn
this neck with a mortal talon

in the midst of space a geranium
lifts its mouths
internal vulvas heavy with fruity roses

the crab
is changed into scent
into pine needles

ardent tides for wildcat joy
washed shores

morning would have to be clawed by a cry
to burn away the alabaster and the frost
to snatch from terror the furthest nebula on the
   brink of death

to free
the adorable frenzy of loving

Dark Archangel

tattered flight of the dried-blood-colored hand of earth

the bittern holds the sky
between the fruit

the shattered trunk of the oak
releases pale suns
which would be the source of light
should morning come

pink is the cave where the apple rustles
quick to the touch of the lively serpent

between the solar arches
on the stems of thirst
aspiration
(in brief gasps the breathing checked)
of the perfect cry

"I consume myself"
says the marvel to the crowd pressing round and
    takes off to the south pursuing the migratory
    flocks

thus the siren
        the pineapple
        the bee make up what memory we have
of this ecstasy

inspired by the triangle
barely touched with pink
like a light perfume
that yet clings
the diverse transformations of the fleece
in the white occupy a triangle themselves

at the torrid zone
at the solar peak of ecstasy
where the veins knot themselves and unknot
where the caresses come tumbling down
there the playful animals stir
the edible feast holds sway

scene to which the pine is hardly indifferent
standing with its needles wildly displayed
having sipped from the spring of a red mouth

further down
the sleek coat of a sable quivers
attending only the caprice of its mistress

and all combines to welcome this warmth
that comes in December
in a frigid land

the pink the infinitely pink
ensures that the gold is reabsorbed in the night and the snow
the pink that teases up a breath
a hardly perceptible breeze
a quiver in the grass betraying the spring

the pink throbs
the loved one encircles it with her arms
with her legs
savors it slakes it
endlessly caresses opens closes it again
drowns it in tears
of fresh water
makes it laugh smile
burst into laughter
break into smiles

around the pink the loved one
unfolds her untamable fur
welcomes its sunsets its dawns
within her mouth as well as within her other mouth
where the nests quicken
the small cries

so that the whole landscape
only exists through the pink
and the loved one
and through her is inhabited by it alone

Portrait of a Girl with Brown Hair

dim lantern face
o lovely face sprung from the dark earth

whom do you light with this red-lipped glance?

what dead man burns with a mortal passion
in the dark circles of your phantom eyes?

to what pain does this tear attest
at which the pools of morning riot

autumn autumn

One

a thousand lovers lift me out of death
pull me from the earth

a thousand lovers who are always one

in fall they leave me taking flight
then reappear
with the leaves

full mouth
leafy sex
summer stirs
in my arms

Anonymous Group (Fourth Dynasty)

see crossing through time
this couple eaten by worms

he solid nearly intact
his left fist clenched on his breast

his right makes fast
a frail hand
which could be that of the little spouse
if her arm (the fingers there
under the armpit having taken root)
did not encircle the man who carries her wholly
minuscule tender burden
birdlike with her ankles eaten away

alone
of all this dismantled wood
this wreckage
undevoured is the gesture of love

Bone Struck Dumb

petrified
upright
great eyes open

the dead man's concubine
holds with crossed hands
an ivory belly

her pubis is a sad triangle
a dried flower

Scarabs

in their glass cases
impenetrable except to the memory of the dead
the scarabs of Egypt keep watch
with closed ranks

of those who pass here none has eyes so quick
he will not perish on the spot
for his sacrilege: go on and exist

now that the desert rules with severity
now that the sun itself is a star merely of dust

Shore Birds

preoccupied
minuscule
most frail themselves since mortal
(the shadow of a footstep in the uproar frightens them)
the sandpipers forage in surf
pick clean of its crayfish its larvae
the surface of terrestrial time
shore always empty where the sea never ceases to shove
    its blades
tribes peoples

Antonioni
(blow-up)

death floats on the surface of the park
green death
the Seurat of death

everything is transfigured the wind the dew
death itself and those who dwell there
its prey in the spring
like the tree and the bud

but the thicket
(numerous bodies sprung from the soil)
thaw barely pronounced
comes alive

mirror image of death in green

Bad Times 1

the water eating the rock and the light space
I do not commit suicide
except every morning and all day
year in and year out throughout the ages
eternity being only the steady flow of cash
    from the holes in the beggar's sack
the interminable time he takes to stuff his soul
and the catastrophic piling up of galaxies
    in the coffers of divinity

Bad Times 2

in these terrible times
the earth weighs on me

like a man buried naked
in the advancing corruption
and the progress of techniques
amid the bitten anger of moles
and the ants

there I am
like a dead man filling himself through his pores
with the very dust of the species

Vietnam, USA

when death strikes who
is the sparrow hawk?

the prey only dies from the sun
napalm pure blade
and the night that ensues

here lies the planet earth
time's shingle smoothed
and sleek

Mission Accomplished

death's lanterns at sea
at dawn
in a flat calm

phosphorous hedgehogs send up yellow signals
    to the bombardiers who return

smooth as the decks for landing
are the shattered villages

the servomechanism is merely memory
and pure serenity the metal

PITT POETRY SERIES

Adonis, *The Blood of Adonis*   Cloth, ISBN 0–8229–3213–X, $5.95/Paper,
ISBN 0–8229–5220–3, $2.95

Jack Anderson, *The Invention of New Jersey*   Cloth, ISBN 0–8229–3168–0,
$5.95/Paper, ISBN 0–8229–52033, $2.95.

Jon Anderson, *Death & Friends*   Cloth, ISBN 0–8229–3202–4, $5.95/Paper,
ISBN 0–8229–5217–3, $2.95

Jon Anderson, *In Sepia*   Cloth, ISBN 0–8229–3278–4, $5.95/Paper, ISBN
0–8229–5245–9, $2.95

Jon Anderson, *Looking for Jonathan*   Cloth, ISBN 0–8229–3141–9, $4.95/
Paper, ISBN 0–8229–5139–8, $2.95

John Balaban, *After Our War*   Paper, ISBN 0–8229–5247–5, $2.95

Gerald W. Barrax, *Another Kind of Rain*   Cloth, ISBN 0–8229–3206–7, $5.95/
Paper, ISBN 0–8229–5218–1, $2.95

Leo Connellan, *First Selected Poems*   Paper, ISBN 0–8229–5268–8, $2.95

Michael Culross, *The Lost Heroes*   Paper, ISBN 0–8229–5251–3, $2.95

Fazıl Hüsnü Dağlarca, *Selected Poems*   Paper, ISBN 0–8229–5204–1, $2.95

James Den Boer, *Learning the Way*   Cloth, ISBN 0–8229–3140–0, $5.95/
Paper, 0–8229–5138–X, $2.95

James Den Boer, *Trying to Come Apart*   Cloth, ISBN 0–8229–3216–4, $5.95/
Paper, ISBN 0–8229–5221–1, $2.95

Norman Dubie, *Alehouse Sonnets*   Cloth, ISBN 0–8229–3226–1, $5.95/
Paper, ISBN 0–8229–5223–8, $2.95

Norman Dubie, *In the Dead of the Night*   Paper, ISBN 0–8229–5261–0, $2.95

Odysseus Elytis, *The Axion Esti*   Cloth, ISBN 0–8229–3283–0, $7.50/Paper,
ISBN 0–8229–5252–1, $3.50

John Engels, *The Homer Mitchell Place*   Cloth, ISBN 0–8229–3149–4, $5.95/
Paper, ISBN 0–8229–5159–2, $2.95

John Engels, *Signals from the Safety Coffin*   Cloth, ISBN 0–8229–3291–1,
$6.95/Paper, ISBN 0–8229–5255–6, $2.95

Abbie Huston Evans, *Collected Poems*   ISBN 0–8229–3208–3, $6.95

Brendan Galvin, *No Time for Good Reasons*   Paper, ISBN 0–8229–5250–5,
$2.95

Gary Gildner, *Digging for Indians*   Cloth, ISBN 0–8229–3230–X, $5.95/
Paper, ISBN 0–8229–5224–6, $2.95

Gary Gildner, *First Practice*   Cloth, ISBN 0–8229–3179–6, $5.95/Paper, ISBN
0–8229–5208–4, $2.95

Gary Gildner, *Nails*   Cloth, ISBN 0–8229–3293–8, $6.95/Paper, ISBN 0–8229–
5257–2, $2.95

Mark Halperin, *Backroads*   Cloth, ISBN 0–8229–3311–X, $5.95/Paper, ISBN
0–8229–5266–1, $2.95

Michael S. Harper, *Dear John, Dear Coltrane*   Paper, ISBN 0–8229–5213–0, $2.95

Michael S. Harper, *Song: I Want a Witness*   Cloth, ISBN 0–8229–3254–7, $5.95/Paper, ISBN 0–8229–5231–9, $2.95

Samuel Hazo, *Blood Rights*   Cloth, ISBN 0–8229–3147–8, $5.95/Paper, ISBN 0–8229–5157–6, $2.95

Samuel Hazo, *Once for the Last Bandit: New and Previous Poems*   ISBN 0–8229–3240–7/$5.95

Samuel Hazo, *Quartered*   Cloth, ISBN 0–8229–3284–9, $6.95/Paper, ISBN 0–8229–5253–X, $2.95

Gwen Head, *Special Effects*   Paper, ISBN 0–8229–5258–0, $2.95

Shirley Kaufman, *The Floor Keeps Turning*   ISBN 0–8229–3190–7, $5.95

Shirley Kaufman, *Gold Country*   Cloth, ISBN 0–8229–3269–5, $6.50/Paper, ISBN 0–8229–5238–6, $2.95

Abba Kovner, *A Canopy in the Desert: Selected Poems*   Cloth, ISBN 0–8229–3260–1, $8.95/Paper, ISBN 0–8229–5232–7, $3.95

Paul-Marie Lapointe, *The Terror of the Snows: Selected Poems*   Cloth, ISBN 0–8229–3327–6, $7.95/Paper, ISBN 0–8229–5274–2, $2.95

Larry Levis, *Wrecking Crew*   Cloth, ISBN 0–8229–3238–5, $5.95/Paper, ISBN 0–8229–5226–2, $2.95

Jim Lindsey, *In Lieu of Mecca*   Paper, ISBN 0–8229–5267–X, $2.95

Tom Lowenstein, tr., *Eskimo Poems from Canada and Greenland*   ISBN 0–8229–1110–8, $4.95

Archibald MacLeish, *The Great American Fourth of July Parade*   Paper, ISBN 0–8229–5272–6, $2.50/Record, $5.95

Judith Minty, *Lake Songs and Other Fears*   Paper, ISBN 0–8229–5242–4, $2.50

James Moore, *The New Body*   Paper, ISBN 0–8229–5260–2, $2.95

Carol Muske, *Camouflage*   Paper, ISBN 0–8229–5259–9, $2.95

Thomas Rabbitt, *Exile*   Cloth, ISBN 0–8229–3292–X, $5.95/Paper, ISBN 0–8229–5256–4, $2.95

Belle Randall, *101 Different Ways of Playing Solitaire and Other Poems*   Cloth, ISBN 0–8229–3261–X, $5.95/Paper, ISBN 0–8229–5235–1, $2.95

Ed Roberson, *Etai-Eken*   Paper, ISBN 0–8229–5263–9, $2.95

Ed Roberson, *When Thy King Is A Boy*   Cloth, ISBN 0–8229–3197–4, $5.95/ Paper, ISBN 0–8229–5214–9, $2.95

Dennis Scott, *Uncle Time*   Cloth, ISBN 0–8229–3271–7, $5.95/ Paper, ISBN 0–8229–5240–8, $2.50

Herbert Scott, *Disguises*   Paper, ISBN 0–8229–5248–3, $2.95

Herbert Scott, *Groceries*   Cloth, ISBN 0–8229–33322, $5.95/Paper, ISBN
0–8229–5270–X, $2.95

Richard Shelton, *Of All the Dirty Words*   Cloth, ISBN 0–8229–3248–2, $5.95/
Paper, ISBN 0–8229–5230–0, $2.95

Richard Shelton, *The Tattooed Desert*   Cloth, ISBN 0–8229–3212–1, $5.95/
Paper, ISBN 0–8229–5219–X, $2.95

Richard Shelton, *You Can't Have Everything*   Cloth, ISBN 0–8229–3309–8,
$6.95/Paper, ISBN 0–8229–5262–9, $2.95

David Steingass, *American Handbook*   Cloth, ISBN 0–8229–3270–9, $6.50/
Paper, ISBN 0–8229–5239–4, $2.95

David Steingass, *Body Compass*   Cloth, ISBN 0–8229–3180–X, $5.95/Paper,
ISBN 0–8229–5209–2, $2.95

Tomas Tranströmer, *Windows & Stones: Selected Poems*   Cloth, ISBN
0–8229–3241–5, $6.95/Paper, ISBN 0–8229–5228–9, $2.95

Alberta T. Turner, *Learning to Count*   Paper, ISBN 0–8229–5249–1, $2.95

Marc Weber, *48 Small Poems*   Cloth, ISBN 0–8229–3257–1, $5.95/Paper,
ISBN 0–8229–5234–3, $2.95

David P. Young, *Sweating Out the Winter*   Paper, ISBN 0–8229–5172–X,
$2.95

All prices are subject to change without notice. Order from your bookstore
or the publisher.

University of Pittsburgh Press
Pittsburgh, Pa. 15260

COLOPHON

This book was set in the Linotype version of Palatino, a typeface designed by Hermann Zapf and named for the Italian Scribe. Heritage Printers, Inc., composed and printed the book directly from the type on Warren's Olde Style antique wove paper. Gary Gore was the book's designer.